Hidden Secrets within the Heart

(Second Edition)

Bessie Bolden

Williams and King Publishers

ISBN: 9798989780419

$\mathcal{D}$edication

I had to write this book because I had so much pain and hurt inside and didn't know how to let it out. I had been carrying all this pain for nearly twenty-four years. I was so scared to tell anybody because when I had confided in someone before, I was punished badly for it. My face always had a smile to hide the pain and hurt.

I cried for days and nights for years, and I still cry even today when I remember, sometimes I still do cry. I look back at my life, and I can see how I overcame everything that was meant to destroy me with the grace of God. I know that many women in the world have experienced what I am testifying about. I used to be ashamed to tell anyone.

I want you to know that I understand every bit of what you're going through because I was ashamed for years. See, the devil had me believing it was my fault. But as I got older, I understood I was too young at the time everything started to happen.

I always thought a father was supposed to protect his children from bad people and love them, not hurt them. I never thought a father was supposed to be the one to take your childhood from you.

Do you want to know what hurt me the most? I was told by the doctor that I couldn't have children because my insides were so damaged from being raped. But look at God! My mom had five girls and two boys and God gave me four boys and three girls. God blessed me with seven children, just like my mother.

To all the women and young girls, you don't have to be ashamed of yourself at all. No matter what, you are beautiful on the inside and the outside. Always remember there is one person who will always be with you. He will never leave your side no matter what you go through, and His name is Jesus Christ. Out of everything I went through, Jesus was with me the whole time. Sometimes, I couldn't see Him, but He was there holding my hands through it all. I was this little girl being abused and feeling like Jesus Christ wasn't there, but He was, and he is still holding my hands. I understand that God protected me and guided me the whole way. When Satan wanted me to feel abandoned by God, Jesus was making a way the whole time. I could have been dead a long time ago, but God kept me here. Jesus Christ is the key to everything. Always pray and keep Him first and He will guide you to the end. Jesus is my King, forever and always.

My love goes out to every woman and girl that have experienced this kind of trauma. You are a strong warrior. Keep your head up and never put it down for anybody. And always keep a smile on your beautiful face.

CHAPTER One

This story is about me, a young lady born with a purpose. However, I wasn't aware of the trials and pain I would have to endure to testify to the goodness of God.

My parents named me Bessie Anderson, and I was born in Deland, FL. I was named after my parental and maternal grandmothers. My mother and father had seven children: two boys and five girls. I was the baby of the family.

When I was five years old, my family moved to Osteen, FL. It was located on the outskirts of Delton, FL. There, I attended a school named Enterprise Elementary.

That's when I realized that life was starting to change. My father had severe heart problems and began taking various medications. Then, my mother had high blood pressure. Things were beginning to take a turn for the worse for my family.

As I got older, life became harder. Nonetheless, my parents kept my siblings and me in church. My father made sure we were in church every day of the week. To other people, it seemed as if our lives were peaches and cream, but they didn't know it was like hell. Just because we went to church didn't mean we had it good. My father was a deacon of Free Will Holiness Church, and we attended ever since I was a baby.

At five years old, I began to witness my father beat my mother frequently. It pained me. I wondered if he really loved her, then why would he do such horrible things to her.

When my siblings and I went to school, he would beat my mother. When we returned, we noticed her black eyes and busted lips that weren't there before.

I would say to myself, *"If there is a God, where is He?"* I begged God to do something. *"Why did I have to watch this at such a young age?"* I always prayed that he would stop beating her.

I was hurt because my father was six feet tall and weighed about 350 pounds. My mom was only a mere five-foot-two. I even witnessed him placing a gun to her head, all in front of me. That night, I was praying for my father to die because I was so tired of being hurt. All the domestic abuse that occurred at home didn't stop us from going to church every day like we lived wholesome lives.

If that wasn't bad enough, by the time I was six years old, I was raped by a very close person that was supposed to love and care for me. It was my father. He told me that if I told anyone, he was going to kill me. I stayed silent because I was scared and believed that he would really kill me if disobeyed him.

Because I was so young, I didn't know what to do. I couldn't tell my mother because I was convinced that he would've killed her and my siblings. My father was a very crazy man.

One day on a Friday, I went to school and tried to talk to someone about what was transpiring at home. I was told by this person that whatever we talked about would stay between us. So, I believed her and explained everything that was going on. By the time I got home, the lady I spoke with had called my father. He called me into the room, and I was scared. He told me to take off all my clothes and he beat me black and blue. I was so sore that I couldn't even sit down that day. I had to stop believing that God existed. I was so hurt that I wanted to kill myself at age six. That person that I thought I could trust didn't change anything. I was still being molested by my father. I remember he would always tell us to go into his room so he could rape us.

One Sunday morning at church, my dad began to beat my mom. Unbeknown to us, by the time church was over Mom had run away. We weren't aware of her absence until church was over when we went looking for her.

All I could do was cry. I was so close to my mom, and my father couldn't do anything because he even knew she was tired. He had gotten so angry that he began cursing. Wow, Deacon Anderson.

So, we left church and returned home. My siblings and I were crying because our mother had just left us. Life, it hurt but he couldn't get me because we know she would've stayed. My dad was going to kill her one day. That night, I was feeling so depressed. I kept thinking why God would let all of this happen.

My sisters and I shared a room, and so did my brothers. Later that night, I fell asleep. Suddenly, I felt somebody pulling on me. As I opened my eyes, I noticed it was my dad. He grabbed me and took me into his room, all while my sisters were asleep. I was weeping, and I couldn't scream because if I did, he told me he'd kill me. He raped me over and over that Sunday night. The next morning, I was ecstatic to see the new ways that life could get any worse. Note the sarcasm.

That day, when my sibling and I returned home from school, Dad had beaten Mom so bad that she tried to overdose with pills. We rushed her to the hospital. The doctor pumped her stomach and notified us that she was going to be okay.

Though life was tough, we did have some good days like when we went fishing and had family cookouts. My dad had two sides to him. We could never visit a friend's house or talk to our friends on the phone. It felt like we were in prison. I enjoyed school because I was afraid to be around my dad. I didn't tell anybody what I was going through, not even my sisters and brothers. They were all I had.

When I got to school one day, my teacher asked me why I wasn't speaking in class. She told me I wasn't acting like my usual self. I just told her that I was okay. I was scared to open my mouth because of what happened the last time.

As life moved on, I turned seven, and things were only getting worse. After my mother left, I kept receiving beatings from my father. Then, a few months later, an envelope came through the mail. My mother was asking my dad for a divorce. I cried because I definitely knew I wouldn't see my mother again. I was the baby girl here alone with my father.

On Monday, I was getting ready for school. That was when my dad suddenly walked into my room and told me I wasn't going to school that day. Then, he left out the room. Tears began to stream down my face because I knew what was about to happen. Being young, I asked God to help me even though I gave up on everything. My sisters and brother left for school, and I was the only one home with Dad.

He raped me over and over and beat me until my body was sore. He reminded me that if I dared to tell anyone, he would kill me. I took a shower, and after that, I went into my room and cried my eyes out. I was so scared for my life, and after my mother left, things went downhill. My siblings came home from school and saw me crying. They asked what was wrong. I was scared because my dad was walking by, looking at me, so I said nothing. That same day, we went to church. My dad acted like nothing happened as he got up in front of the church praying.

Life got even crazier. As we got older, it seemed like we didn't have a life. Dad wouldn't allow us to go anywhere but to church and Grandma's house. I didn't like going there because it was obvious that she didn't care for us. She knew we were getting beat because he would hit Mom in front of her. When I was young, I hated being around my dad's family because he showed them more love than us. He bought for them and never for us. He always made us feel hurt and unwanted.

The only thing my father taught us was how to get what we needed when we didn't have money. For example, going fishing for food and junking for money.

CHAPTER Two

I believed my father had some good in him. I always felt as if he had two sides: one living for God and the other living for the devil.

My freshman year of high school was the time my dad received the divorce papers from my mother. So, we went to court, and the judge granted them the divorce. Within the decree, my sibling and I were to stay with my father during the weekdays, and we could see Mom on the weekends.

The judge made the decree, but my dad wasn't going to agree to it. He didn't care what the order said. It wasn't going down like that. He didn't take us to see Mom. We cried because it had been years since we'd last seen her. A month later, we were driving with Dad, and we happened to see our mother at Wal-Mart. My mom spotted him, and she called the police on him. My dad parked the car in the store parking lot and began spying on her. My dad told us he wanted to kill Mom because she was trying to get us. Suddenly, the police pulled up.

The officers searched the van and found two guns however, my father was properly licensed. The police told my dad he had a restraining order on him filed by Mom, and he wasn't allowed to be around her. The police told my dad if he got caught near her again that he was going to jail. We left the store, and my father was livid. For a deacon, oh my, can he cuss! But he couldn't cuss right at all.

That Sunday came, and we went to church as usual. I didn't feel the same, and I didn't want to be there. I felt like God had let me down because of all the pain and hurt I endured.

One day, I was feeling sick, and we went to the doctor. I had just started my period, and I didn't understand what it was because my mother wasn't around to teach me. The doctor examined me and said my insides were damaged and that I may not be able to have babies.

I couldn't do anything but cry. I was already going through so much as a child. I didn't think there was anything worse that could happen to me. All I knew was I was tired of being hurt all the time.

Back then, I really didn't know what death meant. As far as I was aware, it was when a person went to sleep for a long time.

My father ended up kicking my oldest brother out of the house. He would beat my brother so bad it was almost like he wasn't even his son. We cried for my brother because we were always so close. My dad cussed my brother out and called him names. After my brother left, it seemed as if everyone else wanted to leave too. Then, a few months later, almost all my brothers and sisters ran away from home. It was only one of my sisters, my second oldest brother, and I left in the house.

When that month passed by, my brother and sister graduated from high school at sixteen years old. Even though we were experiencing hard times at home, we still managed to be honor-roll students.

My dad started getting sick, so he made an appointment to see the doctor. We accompanied him during his visit, and once he walked out, he had a funny look on his face. We knew something was wrong, but he didn't tell us anything. Something strange happened that day when he dropped us off and said that he loved us. My father never loved us. After we got out of the van, we went back to school to have fun at the fair.

We knew something was wrong because my dad was always at the bus stop to pick us up. That day, he wasn't, so we had to walk all the way home alone. When we got home, we saw the van in the driveway. The screen was locked but the door was open. So, we began to scream for our dad, and he didn't come. My brother ended up sliding a card through the door, and it opened. We went looking in the room, and he was not there. So, my sisters and I ran to the back door, and we discovered our father's body lying there lifeless. We called 911, and my sisters quickly ran to my friend's house to tell them what was happening. My friend who was a nurse, rushed to our house to check on my father. She confirmed that he was, in fact, dead. In 1999, my dad passed away.

After that, we called our paternal grandmother. She came to the house, and his body was still on the floor when she arrived. The coroner came to pick up my dad's body, and my grandmother tried to sign legal documents for his body. They told her she couldn't because my mom had to because she was the mother of his children.

The next day, my mother received a call informing her about my father's death. She was instructed to come get us because we were still minors. She came crying after she received the news. She couldn't believe he was gone. It was so amazing how my father's family never visited us until my dad passed away. They came over to the house taking everything that didn't belong to them. What made it so bad was that they didn't leave us with anything. What kind of family is that? Luckily, my mother arrived at the house just in time.

That was the happiest day of my life. It was like God had answered my prayers after all that I had gone through. My second oldest brother moved with his girlfriend, and my sisters and I moved in with my mother.

We all stayed in contact with each other when Dad died. I couldn't cry at all, there was too much pain and hate that I had towards him. A few days had passed, and we went to view his body. That day was horrible because my dad's family didn't want my mother there, and they made it known.

She'd endured twenty-three years of abuse from him and bared his seven children. That was a lot of hell. At the wake, my aunt tried to fight my sister, and the police had to come and diffuse the situation. It was crazy with my dad's family. There was so much drama just because they didn't want my mom there. That Saturday, the funeral came, and everything went smoothly. There were many lies concerning my dad's insurance. I think everything was about money when it came to my dad. I felt like it was no love with the family on my dad's side.

My mom got married to a sweet man named Alvin Robinson. He raised us up like his own. He was there for us, loved us and taught us about men.

CHAPTER Three

Because I suffered from an abusive relationship with my father, I hated every man. In 2004, I met a man named Kevin. I was eighteen years old at the time, and I believe he was twenty-nine. I was just trying to find love anywhere. We started talking for a while and began dating by the time my stepdad started getting sick. One night, my mother was screaming and telling us to call 911. We went into the room where my mother was. I witnessed my stepdad die right in front of me. I felt so bad. God, why does everyone I love die?

The paramedics came and tried to revive him, but it was to no avail. They confirmed that my stepdad had passed away. I knew that he was the best thing that ever happened to my mom.

A few days later, we had our stepfather's funeral. After we said our final goodbyes, my mother stayed in her room for days. I could feel her pain because I could see it in her eyes. It took her a while to let go, but she always kept my stepdad in her heart.

A few months passed, I started to feel sick. My attitude had changed. I was getting irritated about everything. Therefore, my sister decided to walk my boyfriend and me to the doctor's office near the house. I saw the doctor, and he told me I was pregnant. I was so happy yet scared at the same time because I was unsure how my mom would feel about it. I was still a baby myself. After a while, I told my mom the news and she was excited.

I was already three months along when I found I that I was pregnant. That's when my life took a turn because I never told my mom what my father did to me when I was young. I finally got a chance to tell her. I wept uncontrollably and so did she. She said if my dad was alive, she would've killed him herself. I was glad I got that off my chest, but Mom was deeply hurt.

A few days later, my mother came home from work with baby girl clothes. She was convinced that I would have a girl. However, my baby was so stubborn that we couldn't determine the sex right away.

My boyfriend and I had stopped talking. His mom got sick and had to be moved to ICU, and I never saw him again. My family and I took over the responsibilities of my baby's father.

My mom never got a chance to go with me to my doctor's appointments. However, there was one day she came home and told me she had taken off from work to go to my appointment. As time went on, my mom was getting sick because of her high blood pressure. She kept taking her medication that she said she wanted to give up. She told us that my stepdad came to her in her sleep and told her when she got her life right, he was coming to get her.

When I was six months pregnant, I found out I was having a girl. I said to myself that I was going to name her Diamond, and I did just that. I promised myself that I would never let anyone or anything hurt her.

One day, my sister, Dorothy, and I left for the store. We left my mom and my other sister, Josette, at home. While we went to the store, Josette was asleep and so was her baby boy. At that time, I was eight months pregnant. The store wasn't even ten minutes away from the house. We found my mom on the bathroom floor crying for help, but the door was locked, and my sister was still asleep. My sister's boyfriend jumped through the window. My mother had so much blood in her eyes. I was crying and praying to God at the same time. *"God, I cannot lose my mother after she's come back into our lives."* I prayed.

We called the ambulance, and they came and took my mom to the hospital near our house in Apopka, FL. I felt like I was losing my mind.

When we got to the hospital, they said we couldn't go into the room. A few minutes later, the doctor let my oldest sister, Dorothy, in the room where my mom was. She was doing okay. She talked to my sister and told her to promise to take care of me and my sister Josette because we were the youngest. My sister said yes, and shortly after that, my mom passed away.

The doctor attempted to bring her back to life, and they made my sister leave the room. I still remember that time as though it was yesterday. In the waiting room, I met a white girl. She said she was sorry for what happened to Mom. She was at the hospital for her mother as well. I never asked for her name because I was crying and upset. However, she told me since that Mom's room was across from her mother's room, she would go and see what was happening. While we

17

were waiting, everyone was also crying and a few minutes later, she came back to inform us that our mother had passed away. The doctor was still in her room trying to bring my mother back.

Shortly after, the doctor called my family into a small room. We already knew what he was about to say. He informed us that he and his team did everything within their power. We all started crying. My oldest sister called my grandmother in Georgia. They told her the news and said she needed to try to get to Florida. My grandmother tried her best to keep the pain inside. My mother, sister, and brother all arrived in Florida within an hour and a half. By the time my grandmother got to Florida, the doctor had already moved my mother's body to another hospital in Orlando. We called my grandmother and told her what hospital we were at. After my grandmother made it to the hospital, that's when all the pain and hurt started again. I was screaming, "Bring my mom back! She is the only parent we have left!"

I was standing there, hoping she would open her eyes. I was pregnant with my first baby. I was asking God to please bring her back. I felt like I was losing faith. I lost my faith in God and didn't believe anymore. I wondered how He could let the person I love so much die right in front of my face.

"Why God?" I prayed.

I knew at the same time that it was not God's fault. My grandmother took my mother back to Georgia, where she was laid to rest.

CHAPTER Four

G od knows, I miss her so much!

I thought about my mother every day. It got to the point that every time I went to sleep, I would wake up thinking she was right there. We went back home after the funeral with a big part of us missing. However, we knew our mother was finally at peace now.

When we returned home, we couldn't sleep at all. We started hearing noises and picked up on strange smells. I was a little scared, but I thought maybe it was our mother watching over us.

At that time, my baby was due in two weeks. Due to all the crying and stress, I was in so much pain. To make matters worse, we also had a hurricane coming. Dorothy drove me to the hospital in the middle of the storm. All the lights were out on the road and fragments of trees were flying everywhere. It was so bad that it was almost impossible to see anything. Lighting even struck throughout the road. We had to drive from Sand Lake Rd. to Rollins Hospital. It was a good thirty-minute drive in those harsh conditions. I was so happy to have my sister there with me. She never left my side.

Thankfully, we made it to the hospital, and they placed me in a room. I was already two centimeters dilated. My sister left and stated she would be right back. I was kind of scared to be there because this was the same hospital my mother died in. I knew my faith had left me because of all I went through. Deep down inside, I knew God would never leave me, so I felt safe.

I started praying to God, *"I'm so scared. This is my first baby, and I don't have anybody here with me."*

I was wishing my mother was there to comfort me. Suddenly, there was that strong smell again that blew under my nose. I got a chilling feeling. I knew that smell, but I thought my mind was playing tricks on me. So, I brushed the feeling off. I was in so much pain, and that smell blew under my nose again. I remembered what the smell was, it was CC Snuff. It was so strong that it had my eyes watering. Then, the aroma filled the room. I was so happy because it was then that I knew that my mom was with me, and so was God.

I began to cry, but it was happy tears. I had a feeling that everything was going to be alright. The next morning, I gave birth to a beautiful little girl that was named Diamond Janah Edwards. I fell so in love with her. I had promised God I would never let anything happen to her.

God gave me a healthy little girl. I lost my mother, but God replaced her with an angel. I cried and cried, wishing my mom could see her. But Mom saw her in the spirit. I felt comforted and safe knowing that she was there with me. Everything was great. I stayed in the hospital for three days before I could return home.

Later down the line, when my daughter was three months old, I moved into an apartment complex called Willow Bend in Pine Hills, FL with my oldest sister. As we started to settle, there was a Spanish guy who lived under us on the first floor. I thought he was so cute, but I didn't pay him any mind. So, I just continued to finish moving the boxes off the truck. As I started to walk up the stairs, there he stood drinking a cup of coffee. He was looking at me, so I said "hello," and he said "hello" back with a smile. I later found out he was in a relationship so, I just kept it moving.

One time we were talking, and I saw that something was wrong with his face, and I asked him about it. He told me that his girlfriend broke up with him because she thought he was cheating on her with me. This was our first time ever talking. We stayed on the steps and talked. He told me about himself, and so did I.

It was amazing. We found out we both believed in God. Even though my faith was off and on, deep down inside, I still believed. A few days later, we started dating and everything was fine. We met each other's families about a month later. After dating for a little while, we got into a disagreement, and he hit me with my newborn baby in my arms.

It's bad when you first meet a person, and they say hitting a woman is wrong. They promised that they would never lay hands on a woman, but it's a lie. I thought about my sister who lived up the street, and I ran to her house. When I got there, she saw my face and asked me what happened. I was still young and didn't want to say anything. She saw right through my response and had a feeling something was wrong.

The next day, he came to my sister's house looking for me, and I was there. We talked, and I went back home with him after he apologized. I was just hoping to God that he wouldn't hit me again.

23

I remember one day I was home and wasn't feeling well. I didn't think anything of it. Days went by, and I still kept feeling dizzy and sick. So, I went to the doctor and found out I was pregnant. I didn't tell my boyfriend right away. God knew I was scared. I would always ask God why this was happening to me. I already went through so much pain.

A few weeks after I found out I was pregnant, I was standing outside talking to one of my boyfriend's friends who lived in the same apartment complex. It was just a friendly conversation. Once my boyfriend spotted us talking, that's when everything got crazy. He started yelling at his friend and cussing at me. He started calling me all kinds of names, so I walked away.

He followed me into the house and started pushing me and hitting me. He knew I was pregnant. He was hitting in my head while I was asking God to please help me. I began to fight back to protect my unborn child. I then grabbed my little girl and ran out of the house, but he followed me outside. There were people outside watching us. The only thing I know is a fist hit me in the face while I had my daughter in my hand.

He struck me so hard that he knocked my teeth out of my mouth. They called the police on him, but he fled. That night, I cried while asking God why I had to endure all this pain to find love. The police wanted me to go to the hospital, but I didn't. I just laid in bed with my baby girl and cried myself to sleep. I didn't see him for a few days until I got a letter in the mail to go to court. A week later, I arrived at the courthouse. The judge called me onto the stand. I was so hurt on the inside, and I had tears streaming down my face. I just wanted everything to be over with, so I lied about everything.

A few days later, I had my baby girl, Jamaya. God blessed me with a healthy baby girl; she was ten pounds and five ounces. I stayed in the hospital for two days. After that, I returned home sore from pushing out a big baby. A few days later, my boyfriend at the time and I got into it again. He hit me in the face knowing I was still sore from giving birth.

I told myself that if I didn't leave, one of us was going to get killed. I just had to get out of there. The next day, I called my sister in Florida and told her I was coming home. My kids' father came back home, and saw my clothes packed and asked what I was doing. I told him that I was leaving and going back home to my family. Also, I let him know I was taking the children with me and that I was tired of all the abuse and name-calling in front of my children.

We fought and fought until he realized I wasn't playing. He ended up taking the children and me to the bus station. It hurt so bad that I needed to leave the man I had been with for seven years. He was my children's father, but I had to leave for the sake of my children. So, my four children and I were on our way from Massachusetts to Florida.

It was hard thinking about starting our life over, but my sister was there waiting for me. My heart was so broken. My baby was almost a month old when I left. She didn't even know her father, but I knew the pain and hurt would end soon.

I finally got to my sister's house and was just happy to be back with my family. However, I was still broken on the inside. As the days passed by, I could feel my happiness coming back. I had to move in with my sister for a while until I got back on my feet. I love my family so much; no matter what I was going through, they were always there for me.

I started going back to church. I attended this one church called The Campground. The first time I went, I could feel the power of God in there. I was at home. I remember meeting a beautiful black queen named Barbara Gaines for the first time. She was preaching service that night and stood me up and told me about something I was going through. What she caught in the spirit was so accurate. I never met her a day in my life, and when she told me this, I broke down crying because everything was true. Prophetess Barbara Gaines understood that I had been through a lot in my lifetime.

.

CHAPTER Five

I always asked myself if God loved me, then why did I have to endure so much pain and abuse. As months passed, I met a person by the nickname of Big Dog. We talked, but my sister I was living with was worried about me because I was the youngest. Plus, I really went through a lot more after my mother left.

I wanted to talk to him, but I also wanted to consider my sister's concerns about me. So, we talked on the phone, even for hours at a time. It was nice and sweet. He told me he had one child when he was just a teenager. I told him I had four children: three girls and one boy. He was cool with it because he wanted more children. One day, he called and said he wanted to meet them for the first time.

That day, my oldest sisters and I got ready to leave, and my brother pulled up at the house. I told him I was going to visit someone, and he asked me who. I told him a man. He then told me that he was coming along, and I refused because he was too overprotective. As we pulled off, my brother followed us. We tried to lose him on the road, but he was persistent. My heart felt like it was going a hundred miles an hour.

We all arrived at the house, and I got out of the car. Everyone was looking at me crazy. Big Dog walked up to me and hugged me. Everyone was looking at us like we were a show. Afterward, we left to go back to my house. My crazy brother told him to ride in the car with him, and I got in the car with my sister. We got back to my house, and he met my family, but like always, my family bombarded him with questions. If you're the baby of the family, everyone is extremely overprotective of you.

After Big Dog passed all the questions, he and I went for a walk in the park near the house. We talked about what we wanted in life, and we had a lot in common. While we were there, we played like little children. It was fun, and I haven't had that much fun in a while. Because it was getting late, we went back to the house so my sister could bring me to take Big Dog home.

About a month later, we began dating. It was Father's Day, and we went out to eat and chilled that whole day. As time went on, I started feeling sick and depressed. Also, I was getting irritated fast. I went to the store and bought a pregnancy test, and it turned out that I was pregnant. I was so scared. I didn't know what to do or say. Big Dog wasn't aware I took a test at all. The next day, I called him over and told him the news. I thought he would've been upset, but he was excited. Soon after, I let my family know that I was having another child. I thought everything was going to be sweet.

We moved in together to raise our children together. Everything was going good until one day, my other children's father called. I had hung up the phone in the middle of talking to him, and Big Dog walked through the door. He started running his mouth.

"Why did you hang up the phone as soon as I walked into the house?" He fussed.

"We were done talking," As soon as I told him I was speaking with my children's father, everything escalated.

"I know you still want him back," He stated accusingly. It was so crazy. I was telling him if it was true, then I would be there with him instead.

I didn't want any problems, so I left the house and went for a walk. My stomach started hurting while I was walking so, I stopped at the park and sat at a table there. I started crying and talking to God, *"I am four months pregnant and going through all this. I am supposed to be happy. I don't want to go through what I went through before."* I sat there and cried until I got a phone call from Big Dog.

"Where are you?" He asked.

"I'm at the park," I replied.

"Why? I want to talk to you," I agreed to meet with him. He walked to the park, and we talked. I told him that I don't do drama because I had been through so much already. I opened up about my past, and he was shocked.

He then said he promised that he wouldn't hurt me, and I believed him. We walked back home and watched a couple of movies that night. My stomach was still hurting, and I got scared. When I woke up the next morning, I called my doctor and made an appointment. It turned out that my blood pressure was high, and my doctor instructed me to get some rest. After the appointment, I went home to help the kids with their homework.

At that time, everything was amazing. My family and I were going to church, and we were enjoying life. But everyone always said the devil knows how to come in when everything is great.

When I got home, Big Dog's friend called him and invited him to hang out at his place. Hours passed, and he didn't return home until one o'clock in the morning. I asked him why he was coming home so late and reminded him that I was pregnant with his child. I also smelled the alcohol on his breath. We got into it.

"I don't want to deal with a mess like this at all," I said, frustrated. He started cussing, and I explained that we had children, and if he wanted to do that, he needed to leave.

"Are you putting me out?" he asked.

"Yes, if it's going to be like this!"

Suddenly, he grabbed me, "If you don't let me go, it's going to be a problem. You know I'm pregnant, and the children are in the room," I warned. "If you ever put your hands on me again, I will hurt you," I threatened.

That night, I slept in another room. While I was lying down, my past had flashed before me. I told myself I would not go back to what I left behind. The next morning came, and Big Dog didn't know what happened. That's what scared me the most.

All that day, I didn't pay him any attention because I was still upset from the previous night. As days and months went on, everything started to get worse. The hitting came, and so did the name-calling. I had fallen so deeply in love with him. I had two more children with him.

In 2013, I got pregnant by him. Come to find out, when the doctor ran some tests on me, I had an STD. As soon as the doctor told me that, my heart dropped. I was faithful to him. I was in a relationship with him for seven years and never hung in the streets or partied at all. I stayed going to church and taking care of my children.

I just lost it. So many thoughts were running through my mind. I wanted to kill him for how inconsiderate he was while I was pregnant with his child. All he did was party and drink. I felt like I was a fool blinded by love. I had been through so much in life, and I didn't think nobody would want me. At least, that's what he told me.

On September 1, 2013, God blessed me with a healthy baby boy. And where was his father? Kicked out of the hospital for smoking weed outside the building. So sad. I was so hurt, but at least my sister was there with me. They always had my back through everything. When I got out of the hospital, my sister, Gensie had made my room look so amazing. But where was my baby's father? Everyone was at my house waiting for my arrival, but Big Dog was nowhere to be found. He came home at midnight. I didn't even have the energy to fight, so I left it alone. The next day, I kicked him out because he wanted to fight and call me names.

I wept and asked God to please help me, *"Lord, why do I have to go through so much pain and hurt when I don't even do people wrong? I just want to be loved. Why can't I find somebody to love me? Is that so hard?"* I cried out to Him.

I was in so much pain because I just had a C-section. My oldest sister stayed at my house to help me. I couldn't do anything because my depression had gotten the best of me. Gensie came over and agreed to look after my baby for a few days. When she left that day, I went into my room and cried until I fell asleep. I was tired of being hurt.

A few months later, I met up with Big Dog. We talked, and he said he was sorry for what he had done to me. At that time, me being me, I was so blinded by love that I took him back. I feared being alone because he always told me I would never find someone better than him, and I believed him. So, I let him move back in, thinking it would be different that time around. After a few months, I found out I was pregnant with his child again. I later gave birth to a beautiful baby boy named Angelo.

In that pregnancy, I went through so much with Big Dog. My self-esteem had depleted, and I wanted to give up on life and kill myself. I got so tired of Big Dog making promises to me about changing, and nothing ever changed. When I went to a doctor's appointment, my blood pressure was elevated. I had to see three different doctors during that pregnancy because it was a high-risk pregnancy. After being released from the hospital, I returned home to tell Big Dog what was going on, and he was nowhere to be found. I waited for his arrival, and he never showed up. He came home the next day drunk. We got into it so bad, and I called him all kinds of names. I'm talking about names that really turned my heart upside down.

We started out living together in our apartment, but because of him taking the money and spending it on his habit. I ended up losing the apartment and storage with all our belongings, including baby pictures. I was so hurt. My children and I had to move with my sister until I got back on my feet. I was so messed up, and I didn't know which way to go. My life had hit the end.

Suicide was running through my mind back-to-back. I didn't even let my family know what I was going through. I smiled on the outside, but many days felt like I was dying on the inside. I was scared to tell my sister, but it was one person

I could always talk to, and they didn't judge me. Her name was Mrs. Barbara Gaines. She reminded me so much of my mother.

Mrs. Barbara Gaines was one of the kindest people you would ever want to meet. She'd encourage you no matter what you were going through. When God made her, He did His thing. She is a woman of God. She and her husband are a powerful and true couple of God. Mrs. Barbara Gaines told me to never give up and that everything was going to be okay.

It took me seven years to let go of everything. I realized God blessed me with beautiful children out of those bad situations.

God, I love you. I want each person who is reading this book to understand that no matter what you are going through, God will always have your back. Even when it feels like he isn't there or far away, he will never leave you nor forsake you. Trust that God will have your back.

I had to learn the hard way because of everything that I endured. Many times, it felt like God wasn't there. I used to ask myself why I should have faith going through all of this pain.

I never stopped going to church, and everything I was going through was being preached in service. I didn't tell anyone, but I knew it was God speaking to me. I started getting my faith back. God had truly blessed me over the years.

My heart was healed. Please, whatever you're going through, don't give up because, at any moment, God can turn your situation around. I'm a living witness. Trust me, God is real.

There were many times I could have been dead, but God kept me here. It's sad when you grow up in a home witnessing abuse and violence. I watched my dad beat my mother all the time. I have watched my father beat her at church, my grandmother's house, and anywhere else he felt like beating her.

I was six years old seeing all of this. Me and my siblings used to cry because we would see my mom with black eyes and busted lips. It hurt me so bad, and sometimes, the only thing you can do is cry. We called the police a lot of times, but nothing would happen. The only thing that happened was we got our butt whipped for calling. My dad beat us with anything he got his hands on.

We went to school sore. We smiled at people, but they really didn't know the truth behind the smiles. We would open up to some of the teachers about what was happening at home. They promised not to tell our father, but they did.

When we got home, he whipped us every time for telling someone we were being hurt. Sometimes, it was so bad, that we couldn't go to school for days.

I used to ask God why we had to go through so much pain watching my mom trying to kill herself. My mother had been with my father for twenty-four years. That was twenty-four years of hell she endured. I love my dad's family dearly, but I just don't want anything to do with them.

They knew what was going on from the beating and raping. They never did anything for us while my dad was alive, not until he died. When he died, they left us nothing at all. They came into the house like everything there belonged to them.

My father's family was very selfish. I remember when my dad died when we went to view the body. His family didn't want my mom there and my sisters. My father's sister slapped my sister when we went to view the body. Then they tried to fight my mom, but forgot that we were the ones who went through hell being beat and raped when my dad was alive.

We endured all of that and nobody from that side of the family experienced the hell we went through. Only when they needed something, we would see them. God brought us through all this, and He used the bad experiences to make my family strong.

Even though we went through all that, God never gave up on us. He had a way of escape for us and was always on our side. I will always love God for the rest of my life. I owe him for taking care of us through all the hurt and pain. Most of the time, I wanted to give up, but then, I would remember how God never gave up on me.

It's so amazing how God did things for me when I was living up north in Farmington Hills, Michigan. I went to jail for something I didn't do. My children were taken away from me. My oldest daughter was two years old, and my son was still a newborn. When the police came, they took my children. I even asked if my friend could look after them, and they said no because she wasn't family. I had never been in trouble because the only thing I could think about was my babies. So, I sat in jail that night, and I was released the next morning. I asked them where my children were, and they told me that they were in the custody of the Department of Children and Families (DCF). I cried and cried. I was so mad at God at that time, but I realized God does everything for a reason.

The judge had me do numerous things to get my children back. I told him all of that didn't have anything to do with my case. However, he said it was just the requirements of the state of Michigan. I went home, and day and night I cried because I didn't know who had my children. The judge had given me visitation rights on Fridays for an hour. God knew that it hurt me because my children didn't know who I was. God knew it was killing me.

There were so many times I wanted to kill myself because my children weren't with me. But God wouldn't let me, He had other plans.

Months passed by, and I did everything the judge ordered to get my children back. I never told my family that I had my kids taken away, I only told them I went to jail. My sister had called me and said she and my other sister were coming up north to visit me. I was so sad because my children were not living with me, and I didn't know how to tell her that. I started making so many excuses as to why they couldn't visit. My efforts were useless, though. Debbie and Gensie had already bought bus tickets to come to Michigan. I was scared. They said they were leaving out that afternoon and they would be in Michigan that Saturday morning.

A few days later, it was a Thursday, and I had to go to court. I had done everything the judge had asked. I passed all my tests and completed the program. So, the judge called me to the front, and I knew God was with me. The judge informed me that my children were back in my custody. I cried, and my heart dropped. My oldest daughter was two years old when she went in and three years old when I got her back. My son was nine months when he went in, and two years old when he came out.

What amazed me is that God is an on-time God. On Friday afternoon, I had my children back. God had my back and my front the whole time and never left my side. My sisters got to meet my son. They had never seen him, only in pictures. I had an amazing time when they visited. God had planned everything so well, and everything worked out in my favor.

God is an awesome God. If we just hold on and put Him first, He will work everything out.

CHAPTER Six

He worked everything out to the point that one night, I got on my knees, and I prayed. I told God the next man He sends to me, I want him to be my husband. I didn't just want a boyfriend; I wanted a husband. I also told God what kind of man I wanted. So, I left it. Just like that. I stayed going to church with my kids and working.

About two years later, I met someone. Sometimes you must wait a little while because when God does it, He does it right. We must be patient. So, me and this other person started talking and going on dates. We had a lot of things in common. Our birthdays are in the same month, and we both share the astrological sign, Leo. When I got on my knees that night and I told God what kind of man I needed, He did it. God gave me a family man.

What I mean about that is that I have kids, and not only that, I have seven kids and this man accepted all of them. I'm like,

"Where has this man been all my life?" This man puts a smile on my face. We talked for a while but on August 19, 2016, we became a couple. I felt like I was living a dream. I never thought I would love again or fall in love again, but I did. He swept me off my feet. He is an amazing dad to my kids. I feel like the luckiest woman in the world! Yes, we have our days when we bump heads, but it's nothing our love can't fix. I felt like a little girl in the candy store. Me and my love were together for a few years, and on December 6, 2022, we got married. It was one of the best days of my life. I married my best friend. He knew everything I went through, and still, he asked me to be his wife.

When God gets His hands in the situation, He does it right every time. I say to everyone who is reading this book, don't give up. Your life has a purpose. I had to learn that for myself because I was a person who wanted to give up. I have a husband who prays for me more than he prays for himself. My husband taught me so much and I thank God for him.

What God did for me, he will do it for you. Don't give up on God because He won't give up on you. God loves you more than you know. Just hang in there because He knows what we need. God knew I was missing a piece from the puzzle of my life. My husband was the missing piece of the puzzle of my life. When God connected that missing piece, it became an amazing, completed puzzle - full of love and happiness. My husband is my other and better half of me. God had blessed me with everything I needed.

> ***Thank you, God, for loving me and never giving up on me. My life is a blessing.***